ALL
I WANT IS
A WALK-ON
PART

LIVRES
DC
BOOKS

Cover design by Gerald Luxton.

Designed and typeset in Palatino
by DCAD Enterprises, Montreal.

Printed and bound in Canada by AGMV Marquis.

Distributed by General Distribution Services.

Copyright © LaMonte Palmer, 2000.

Legal Deposit, Bibliothèque nationale du Québec
and the National Library of Canada, 3rd trimester, 2000.

Canadian Cataloguing in Publication Data.

Palmer, LaMonte, 1924 -
All I want is a walk-on part

ISBN 0-919688-60-8 (bound) - ISBN 0-919688-58-6 (pbk.)

I. Title.

PS8581.A56A84 2000   C811'.6   C00-900756-3
PR9199.3.P3235A84 2000

DC Books, 950 Decarie, Box 662, Montreal, Que., H4L 4V9

All I Want Is a Walk-On Part

LaMonte Palmer

Contents

11. Hell's Gate — Kenya
12. Conversations with Felix
14. Dinner at The Addis Ababa Hilton...
16. African Monochrome
18. Predators and Scavengers
20. Thorn Trees (Acacias)
22. Elephant Spotting — Kenya 1986
24. Stardust
26. Jeannie in Athens
27. A Sixties Poet in the Nineties
28. Bed Games for a Married Couple
30. The Game
31. Lovers' Quarrel
32. Compost Blues
34. Conjugal Argument
36. Christmas Pantomime
38. Misconceptions and Psycho-Babble
40. *Folies Rouges*
41. On the Last Day of the World
42. Quarrel of Lovers
43. Irish Cleaning Woman
44. Jeannie in My Town
46. Age Gap in the Jockey Club
47. Night Song
48. Leaving
49. Missing
50. When You're Gone
52. *Femme du Loup* and Mother Goddess

54. Canadian Spring
55. Where Do Babies Come from, Felix James?
56. Four Haiku Poems
58. Requiem for a Lost Prairie
59. Doctor's Office
60. Father, Death Called for You and Me
62. Death and Other 'D' Words
64. Hospital Duty Doctor
66. Prairie Scene 1968
68. Southern Alberta Drought — 1934
70. Reluctant Guest
72. Winds from the Past — Waterton 1997
74. Wyndham at the Breast
76. Young Tragedian
78. Last Retreat
79. Spring's Prairie Oratorio
80. All I Want Is a Walk-On Part
81. Cottage Phantoms

Acknowledgements

The author and publishers gratefully acknowledge the support of the Canada Council for the Arts and SODEC for their publishing programs.

"Jeannie In Athens" was selected for publication in *Vintage 96* published by The Canadian League of Poets. "Prairie Scene 1968" won third prize in the Hope, B.C. Poetry Contest. Many of these poems have been published in sundry Canadian magazines.

The Canada Council for the Arts SINCE 1957 | Le Conseil des Arts du Canada DEPUIS 1957

SODEC
Québec

To Jean, my wife...

Hell's Gate — Kenya

We saw a baby zebra, lost,
snuffling for his mother and the herd,
(whose numbers were a shield.)
We hoped he'd find them or those wide eyes
wouldn't see another dawn.

We had noticed lion pug marks in the sand,
heard the wild dogs yelp.
Vultures, wordless Jeremiahs,
circled, foretelling doom.

What to do? We were helpless.
We watched, and then drove on.
He would stumble around till dusk,
among stalking shadows.
Little one, you will not outrun the night!

It was years ago, and now,
I sometimes wake, in the dark, sweating.
I think of that zebra colt
down on the valley floor
as night closes in.

All I Want Is a Walk-On Part

Conversations with Felix

What's this, small friend?
Eyebrows like a Hebrew prophet,
eternally surprised that no one understands,
you want to tell a brave and solemn tale,
all marvellous vowels and earnestness?
Would you like to pass on Heaven's gossip
from where you came just thirteen weeks ago?

Clever thinkers now reject such notions,
and yet, the wonder that you came at all
would suspend an atheist's disbelief.
Did you meet Yeats? Or Moses Mendelssohn,
the old philosopher, who also had a grandson Felix?

I understand so little of your talk,
only the joys and sorrows of your changing face,
uncoordinated symmetry of arms and legs
ready to conduct four tone-deaf orchestras.

New earthlings bring the scent of other worlds,
dew-drenched angel wings,
breath as light as semiquavers
from any scherzo Mendelssohn could write.

Fingernails, ten perfect haiku poems
each written on a pin head....
You speak and I revel
in the miracle of little boys.

Dinner at The Addis Ababa Hilton During the Famine

December 1985

Candles glowed through the burgundy.
Down from the silk wall-carpets
gazed Haile Salassie's chained cheetahs
giving the soup course ambience.
British airmen, tired and hungry,
had dropped ninety tons of maize
to walking corpses who stumbled back
to feed the starving children.

The chef's fish, world renowned, was served
with shrimp, and most delicate ginger sauce.
The U.S. Aid director took three helpings.
Too busy to see refugees, he was on duty
eighteen hours a day, for consultation
in the dining room, or bar.

Der Grosse, the German count
waddled wheezing from the buffet,
with his nth red meat platter.
His friend, the jolly Canadian nurse
admired his performance,

matched him beer for beer, rib for rib,
loin for loin.

Salad brought talk of the other hotel,
better food, but a mediocre swimming pool.
Cubans and Russians there
had brought in champagne, caviar and vodka.
They were loading Ilyushin jets with lambs,
bound for Russia in exchange for tanks
to crush Ethiopian rebels.

All I Want Is a Walk-On Part

African Monochrome

In Dar Es Salaam, (Haven Of Peace),
one night I paced unlit streets
past baobab trees and flaking paint.

Sudden rain brought out termites.
I stepped into a doorway. When they cleared,
moon's lantern tried to light the town
and me in my alcove, not alone.
A shabby man who'd sensed me long before
blended with black shadows.

He couldn't see me in the feeble light,
nor moon earth. Her reflecting eye
had no more sight
than those blank moonstones
that gently stared at me.

I paused there to talk with him,
surprised by his serenity.
It seemed he'd groped his way
past hunger, no roof,

and the wish to see things beautiful,
come into a secret world

seen only by his milk-white eyes,
where his step was long and sure.

I slipped some money in his palm,
for the peace he had,
I couldn't buy or beg,
and wondered if his alabaster eyes
could sense the rage on my white face.

Predators and Scavengers

Vultures range the deserts and savannas
like medieval bards following wars.
Weightless on lifting air they watch
couplings of predator and prey.

Hyenas razor out a gazelle,
when driven off by lions, wait their turn —
Nature's laws allow no waste of food,
buzzards eat, then beetles clean the bones.

Stone-age man drove off the scavengers;
with crafted hand-axe broke the skull,
split the bones for brain and marrow,
but dreamed he hovered high above the birds,

dreamed of icy seas and other lands,
created gods who made new laws for man
and gave the world to his creators.
But mankind wanted more, the moon, the stars.

Now satellites guide planes as fast as sound
to cut communications, 'take out' bridges,
trap and slaughter ninety thousand men.
Reporters — modern bards — and buzzards watch.

In their hotels reporters earn their loot,
write in praise of winners' deeds and gloat,
while birds pounce on the losing dead and glut
themselves until they cannot fly.

All I Want Is a Walk-On Part

Thorn Trees (Acacias)

In my Nairobi garden,
pinched and claustrophobic light
ricochets from leaves
as big as bullhide shields.

Half century ago,
Englishmen surveyed the wilderness,
dug wells, created Eden
on this African plateau.

Levantine figs, Asian mangoes,
vie with English rose,
palm trees, birds of paradise,
dizzying scents and hues
fenced high by bougainvillea.

Almost concealed,
one tattered desert thorn tree
stands near a frangipane
— bag-lady at the vicar's tea.

Out on the savannah,
light runs straight as a Masai spear.
Acacias grow, five thousand miles across a continent,

from the Congo and the Mountains Of The Moon,
like tattered umbrellas at sidewalk cafes.

Ten million years these trees
bestowed a poor and grudging shade,
and food, small clustered leaves,
each no bigger than a termite.

Giraffes and desert antelope
snaffle out these morsels,
risk stiletto points that pierce
heart or skull, or craft a crown of thorns.

Now our well runs dry,
pumps break. Pansies and petunias,
gardenias and camellias
die and drift away,
as the thorn calls his tribe in from the plains.

All I Want Is a Walk-On Part

Elephant Spotting — Kenya 1986

To Sandor, my grandson

It was your birthday on the Masai Mara,
and you were elephant spotting,
which meant peering through my binoculars.
The animals weren't needed for the sport.

But you saw elephants close up, next day,
great trumpeting, glacial age hold-outs,
yawning lions, bored with playing jungle kings.
Then, as we rested near a fence,
a rubbernecking ostrich three-toed up.

We were just as nosey as he,
but you went up close,
only wire between you,
and it wasn't you who was afraid.
but that chicken-hearted bird.

It's hard to say who began the race,
but you both started running down the line
until he stopped, dragged feathers in the dirt,
ran in circles — avian breakdown.

Then you ran the other way,
and that overgrown turkey hated it,
raced you back, and threw another wing-ding.
No wonder he'd been grounded.

On the way home you asked, "Are elephants afraid?"
"They're afraid of nothing."
"I wasn't afraid of the ostrich, Grandpa."
"No. After all, you've spotted elephants, seen lions,
and turned six."

Stardust

To my wife, the slim girl

In nineteen-forty-three
straight over the dance floor
past dizzying scent of girls and would-be Spitfire heroes,

past lanterns, white streamers and red balloons,
I walked a firm line to a slim girl,
and whatever future war would leave.

Like a practiced gigolo
a silver sax was sweet-talking *Stardust*,
till suddenly the tune became a virgin
on a honeymoon first night.

Come dance, slim girl, before the saxophone
remembers that he married
and dumped that song three times,
and only now sees what he missed.

Let's be quick before the music fades,
arpeggios are dancing,
supported by the bass and drum.
Magic held too long becomes pedestrian.

It was beautiful that night:
music, shapely satin gowns in lantern light,
airmen in their dress blues.
Even me, young, unravaged yet by Time,
with that lovely girl, dancing....

Jeannie in Athens

Was that you, how long ago
sitting in the *Plaka*
under the Acropolis
and Aegean sun?

Persians stormed the wooden walls
while Greeks hurled down stones,
but I wasn't watching them,
I was looking at the sun on your face.

Pericles hired stone cutters,
rebuilt Athens with his oratory.
I didn't hear his words,
only your laughter.

I should have photographed Alcibiades,
splendid in his bronze chariot,
but I was taking pictures of you
in your yellow silk dress.

Now the photos fade,
dust clouds corrode the sun,
but some things do not change:
dead Greek heroes and the sound of your laugh.

A Sixties Poet in the Nineties

If you weren't just bitch enough
to skewer my pretensions,
prod a finger at my fat,
if you didn't laugh at my bad jokes,
(I gave up on the good ones)
if a smirk didn't belie your frown
when I say something 'off color,'
then I'd walk out and slam the bloody door —
(not the glass one)
and never never never
come back
until lunch.

All I Want Is a Walk-On Part

Bed Games for a Married Couple

So! You turn your back to me
my dreaming beauty,
bride of many honeyed moons.
Why should I care?
An artist would gladly paint your back,
and hang it in the most important spot
at his show. I
admire your back,
but your front is more interesting.
Adam saw Eve's back,
but when she displayed the forbidden fruit
she faced her future role.

Now I hear a small, female snore,
cute, but an embarrassment to you.
"Dear, you're snoring."
The barrier is razed
as you turn your softer side to me.
Now I feel your breath,
like cirrus clouds,
urged along by heaven's choirs.
My gentle arm around your waist
is like the dance when we first met,

and now I'll also sleep.
Unknowing, you've invited me to dreamers' land,
though not your dreams,
a rougher land, but suitable for me.
Tomorrow we shall meet again,
lying back to back. Game over,
ready to face the day.

The Game

I honed my skills to gain the prize,
or make a decent show,
felt guilty all my life,
for rules I broke, or didn't know,
and for mistakes, paid the price.

The game was nearly done before
I learned that skill was not admired,
only the slick pretence of skill.
There were no rules,
and for mistakes, nobody cared.
There never was a prize at all.
No one was keeping score.

Lovers' Quarrel

After the hurled words, like cannon shot,
silence fell —
snow falling on a grave.

Words can glibly tell of famous victories,
but not the bleakness of a bare sea
when a happy ship slipped beneath the ice,

to lie in murky canyons,
unseen except by bulge-eyed fish
and shadows passing from another day.

Truth's missiles caused the wreck.
Long days and longer nights
dragged by.

He, who had forgotten laughter
now remembered hers.
In cloistered sleep she dreamt of his caress.

Sea voyages seem eternity.
By chance one night their bodies touched,
their wounds bathed by tears.

All I Want Is a Walk-On Part

Compost Blues

My wife throws coffee grounds into the compost.
I tell her, they make the plants nervous
and get into the food chain.
I have to give the violets valium,
adjust the *prozac* dose for petunias
so they don't hang their heads.

Tree roots absorb caffeine.
Quaking Aspens had a nervous breakdown
this year, shakier than ever.
The weeping willow's on a crying jag.

Ants in the peonies
run round like old news reels,
and birds that eat them sing all night.

An epileptic skunk
throws fits in the flower beds,
comes out smelling like a rose.
Alley cats walk tightrope on the clothesline.
Wolves, drawn to where the action is
surround the house, cut off exits.

Crouched inside
we percolate the final washed-out dregs,
tortured by withdrawal shakes.

Conjugal Argument

Nice-girl words and phrases,
heat-seeking missiles,
take out my super gun, disrupt communications.
I'm left, like Sadam,
bad-mouthing you, losing a war I started.

My Air Force sergeant drilled me in war vocabulary,
phrases to blast a Hun in his tank,
make Italians give up without a fight,
win a forties war. But minus Sunday school language,
a battle with a sweet-talking wife is lost.

If God had sent my sergeant to kick Adam out,
he would have yelled:
"Get your bare buns and that stupid
fig leaf out of that garden.
Try a banana leaf, bozo,
And take that snake-happy, forbidden-fruit bat with you."

More forcefully, the Lord said: "Get thee hence."
Then He added the nasty bit.
Now Adam must earn his bread
by the sweat of his brow,
joining the unskilled labour class.

When Moses got water from the rock and took the credit,
God said something like:
"Moishe, what maybe were you thinking?"
and made him wander in the wilderness for forty years,
a punishment all married men will find familiar.

But you could give the Lord and my drill sergeant
post-doctorate courses,
confound, in a polite voice, the tongues
of Pharisees and Sadducees,
no expletives to delete.
Never a "shut up you stupid bastard"
crosses your lips.

It makes a fellow curse!

Christmas Pantomime

We laid out the *crèche* and lit the tree,
when mother pointed to the window,
Santa Claus! We all saw him,
then, only reflected coloured lights,
and we couldn't wait to tell father.

My brother found his tracks next day.
Santa must have been like father,
proud of his small feet.
He might have followed in father's footsteps.

Next summer, we found a Santa mask
and scarlet touque in the wardrobe,
but by this time it didn't matter.
Santa was out of the closet.

✥

In Greece, twenty five years later,
I was a diplomat, a wise man from the West.
His Excellency asked me to play Saint Nick
at his children's party.

Overdressed and overstuffed,
I took enchanted kid upon my knee.
I was ready to do *White Christmas,*
when my infant son toddled up,
climbed up and stared
past the rouge
the virgin wool eyebrows and sheepish beard,
the Emperor's new clothes,
poked a finger in my eye
and loudly accused, "Da-da!"

Unmasked! Shamed!
Acting career in ruins!
Herod's hostility toward the innocents.
Was it diplomatic to climb an ambassador's chimney?
When does the next donkey leave for Egypt?

Dad got off easy.

All I Want Is a Walk-On Part

Misconceptions and Psycho-Babble

We promised each other
at our next early breakfast,
getting to the truth over decaf.,
false self image, and egg substitute,
we'd discuss being two separate persons
and not just a single pair,
(indistinct identities),
but we forgot to set the alarm,
lay in bed together,
wrapped in *NutraSweet* dreams,
and missed the rendevous.

We tried to fathom
who's who, then and now,
Abelard-Eloise,
Hermes-Aphrodite,
you-me,
but talked in mythic tongues
mystifying all interpreters
and confounding marriage counsellors.

One of us will die
with intact misconceptions,

(blurred edges of identity)
and the other will not know
which one is left.

Folies Rouges

On the drive to open the cottage
we saw a new red roof,
red as a baboon's bum, florid as a ruby
in a belly dancer's belly button!

In midsummer at a church bake sale,
we met the red-roofed couple.
She tossed back a lock of lovely hair and said,
"It embarrasses him, poor boy, but I like it."
I looked at her and liked it too.

In the last week of September,
we drove the road again. Surprise!
The roof no longer looked so red,
and trees dressed up for autumn's fête,
like sumac, scarlet clad, who bitched and sniped,
"Red? Well, not really, my dear.
That roof's pale pink, compared to me."

But when winter comes, trees shed their seven veils
and hide their nudity behind the conifers.
Then the roof looks inappropriate
as a belly dancer on the cardinal's lap,
at a church bake sale.

On the Last Day of the World

All the icons have been broken,
houses split and dreams seep out,
bone caves crushed to earth,
rings of stones, a million years
of prayers and tears, until
the fire burns out in the last hearth.

I would have said we have seen
twenty thousand days go dancing by,
and now the fiddler plays no more,
but it's too late for words —
a billion words already squandered,
treaties shredded, tongues confounded.

People run around demanding
how could this be?
Who's to blame?

It's too late for blame,
so I clutch your hand
and wait,
on the last day of the world.

All I Want Is a Walk-On Part

Quarrel of Lovers

As I walked through the door
your silence hit me like a missing life,
an unheard scream.
We knew what lay between us....
Should wars end
like a newsreel of Hiroshima's flash?

Your noise-proof wall could not be breached
barricaded in your soundless land
volume turned up full mute
a woofer in my guts

I crept out, my love crumpled on the floor
like discarded pajamas,
a love that once had filled the room
the house, the town,
could fill a black hole where a red giant
imploded a universe
and left a white dwarf
in a hushed and silent sky.

Irish Cleaning Woman

She came in, jaw set for a fight,
prepared to dislike the *Memsahib*.
The dislike was instant and mutual when
she sneered at my wife's line-up of cleansers
and glanced knowingly at me.

Her eyes said, "It must be awful with her."
I was, I guess, expected to choose.
She took off her boots
checked to see if I could look up her skirt.
Snagged cotton stockings, unclean bloomers,
and inner thigh varicosities.

They locked horns in the kitchen
and by now they had tails and cloven hoofs.
I sided with the devil I knew,
but we badly needed a cleaning woman,
so I promised to buy a *Dust Pirate,*
and *Missus Murphy's* cleaning fluid.
She would come back Thursday!
She never appeared.
She thought she was the only devil in town!
But there are a legion more
if you sneer at their cleaning equipment.

All I Want Is a Walk-On Part

Jeannie in My Town

Half a century ago I brought you to my town.
You were so lovely the local beauty queen
went home and broke her looking glass.
Two men left their wives to join the Foreign Legion.

(I should have brought you in a golden coach
pulled by a dozen silver stallions,
at least a golden Cadillac, but I lacked gold,
had silver only for the Greyhound bus.)

Soon, the village belle retrieved her crown,
replaced the mirror, bought a stunning dress.
In Calgary, the two Beau Gestes got drunk,
next morning, sheepish, dragged their tails back home.

Now, golden oldies, we return, two old survivors,
unseen by contemporary beauties
and grandsons of the would-be legionnaires,
smug in the accustomed comfort of our days,
I sometimes wish that we were back there, then,

youthful, lettuce crisp, among those boys and girls,
untried as fledgling eaglets,

glancing shyly at each other,
the best of both our lives out there ahead,
waiting to be discovered.

Age Gap in the Jockey Club

A girl glanced at me, and pranced
up toward my table like a yearling mare,
lavishly exuding youth,
and granted me an unearned smile —
orthodontic cyclorama!

But I, put out to pasture,
scratched her from the starting gate,
and saw her forty seasons down the track,
long in tooth, whining whinny,
grey switching pony tail.

Then I felt my oats, no longer wild,
remembered taking fillies for a canter,
and relented, offered her a chair,
and looked this gift-horse in the mouth.

Take from me half the forty years I dumped on her,
and at the Day-Dream Stud Olympics she
would have testosterone squirting from my ears,
and make me blow the steroid test.

Night Song

How can I sing the night
unless I know the tune?
Only a lonely bird or mother whale
can read the notes on the wind's staves
and hear the savage harmony
breaking on the shore.

I could tell you the words.
They were breathed into my ear
in an hour of scent and touch
by moist lips and trembling tongue
when I hungered for her,
when she had gifts she wished to give.

But the tune comes from another place.
Perhaps a hermit in the wilderness
caged in prayer and visions
hears its descant on the nightly wind.

Shadows whisper only words to me,
so how can I sing the night?

All I Want Is a Walk-On Part

Leaving

I'll go on ahead of you
along the rim, past the upturned plough,
by the weather-silvered gates
and old barn site.

Rusting cans clot the glade
where wild columbines
drank petalfuls of sun.

I'll take the downward path,
edge the burnt forest
to Charon's landing,
coin in hand to pay the toll.

They say the ferry wafts the smell of fear,
is silent as the river and as black.
I'll wait over there for you
as long as memory of our first touch.

Follow me only when you must.
I'll be where the others disembark,
and hope we'll find each other
somewhere in the dark.

Missing

The perfumed closet smells of mould,
every dress, once touched each day
now sags in the dark.

Suits of former gala nights
now shoved aside or snatched at dawn,
the lofty double mirror pushed back
face against the wall.

Unseen beings tiptoe through the bedroom.
Half the queen-size bed is smooth,
one pillow laid out flat and cold,
the other wet and twisted.

When You're Gone

The bedroom we decorated
with our dreams upon the wall,
reeks like empty motel rooms,
and yesterday's strangers.

Insecure spirits stir,
bump into the love seat,
whisper, "She's not coming back,
strip off the wall paper."

On the knave side of the queen size,
the tune we danced runs through my head,
modulated to a minor dirge,
major keys reactivate the ghosts.

Meals dealt out like solitaire,
win some, lose some, pass the time,
microwave can't warm my feet or soul.
Days are short, nights wander.

Flowers that danced for you
in sunlight and in wind,
won't raise their eyes to me.
I have no words they understand.

I miss the cadence of your laugh,
the way you touch my hair,
how you squint your eyes
with that conspirator's smile.

I dreamed our house had blown away,
I woke with you there in a tent,
we looked around that canvas room,
and shared conspiratorial smiles.

Femme du Loup and Mother Goddess

I caught sight of you, wolf woman,
coming from the corner of my dream,
wilting lilies in your hair.
I protested, "Go away. You reek
of rotting funeral wreaths,
corpses bleached in candle light,
a mockery of one whose counsel I have lost."

"Was it you who suckled twins upon the Tiber?
Where are your legions now?
Scattered piles of bones
can never form a phalanx,
  — witch, of many guises, and a lupine heart."

Once, fevered and delirious,
before sulpha drugs,
I smelled the musty breath of fresh dug graves.
A giant bat or lobo lurked just beyond my sight.
My mother stayed up three nights
soaking my infected arm.
I heard her take a broom
and drive the creature out.

Suddenly I glimpsed the morning star,
heard dawn come creaking up the stair.
Mother slept, while I sat up and watched the sun
weave a yellow garland for her hair.

Canadian Spring

Ice bound spectres upon the lake
shuddered and began to move.
Spring was late and dark there by the edge
where big pines and prehistoric stones
guarded the sanctity of pagan souls.
Primal memories stirred,
glimpses of the old gods shifted
like mammoths in the arctic ice.

Down among the tamaracks
fiddle ferns unrolled beside the grey stream.
Unblinking trout watched the dragonfly
kick from his cocoon, winter-worn,
all knees, elbows, glorious wings.

Winter's ghostly palm still pressed
bone-white upon the mountain rim.
Old spirits sighed. Eighty miles of river ice
smashed and ricketted down the gorge,
cursing the gods, jeered by honking geese
heralding spring.

Where Do Babies Come from Felix James?

For a grandson, born in Australia

This one landed from a moon walk,
scalpel shortcut from his capsule,
when faulty systems
plagued the launching pad.
He lurked along the lunar dark side,
floated free beside the Southern Cross,
until they cut the life-line,
hailed re-entry, and the nursing sister
supervised his splash-down.

Helpless innocent, he
soon programs his environment:
starts anxiety workshops for adults,
alerts the early warning watch,
renounces silence, food, sleep,
(nocturnal walkabout parents)
then takes the breast and 'blisses out,'
— massacre of the experienced.

We fret for his future,
while he strolls antipodean stars.

All I Want Is a Walk-On Part

Four Haiku Poems

Winter moon
shines into bedroom—
old man shudders

Around the lake's edge
ice lingers
like wallflowers at a dance

I wouldn't have plucked
you off the wall
if you hadn't been a flower

You dream of unicorns with my face
I dream of nymphs with your body

All I Want Is a Walk-On Part

Requiem for a Lost Prairie

Once, out of willow creeks and coulees
darted wild nocturnal mares,
through meadowlark nests and native grass,
past sacred Blackfoot burials
toward the mountains tilting to the sky.

Now the prairie's turned and sown,
mustangs broke to harness,
or dog food.
Coyotes howl across the soil drifts
and mounds of unsold wheat.

Tribal paths lost, campfires gone,
legends winnowed on park benches,
talk of lances, buffalo, great hunts,
wild horses remembered
only in the sun dance.

Blackfoot muffled drums pound out the requiem.
That world is gone and it's too late,
too late to watch the bounding mares,
to walk barefoot through ancient prairie grass
among the moonlit ghosts.

Doctor's Office

Her hat perched like a little bird
searching in vain for crumbs.
I gave her truth's vinegar:
a massive stroke — he didn't die.

She looked to me for hope — none.
I wished she'd weep — I would have too,
touched her hand, awkwardly patted her arm,
instead, nurse brought tea.

No lightning split the sky,
no stone rolled back,
her husband wasn't unalive.

She sipped the tea,
looked at leaves outside turning brown.
Hard centuries teach such women
to hide their pain.

"He never said or did an unkind thing."
I didn't add, "Now he'll say nothing at all."
She wanted to shout her next question:
"Why? Why him?"

Father, Death Called for You and Me

i

When Death first called for you,
capering up the dirt path from the east gate,
a bow and fiddle jutting from his pack,
you were in the fields away.
Mother, trembling, fed him at the doorstep,
took back the cleaned plate and said, "Now git!"

Later when we lived in town, Death called again,
found you home, your woman gone,
taken to God's gusty palace.
You gave him the bum's rush,
"I have affairs to settle.
Come back in seven months
in the dark of night,
but don't show up like an old tramp
or I'll set the dogs on you."

So you picked your time,
to go to her up there
above the mountain snow.

You found her on a heavenly catwalk
where the newest angels strut their reborn youth.
You saw the shyness that you loved,
and all her fear had gone.

ii

Death called twice for me,
but wizard doctors outwitted him,
and he skipped down the path.
Father, you knew him well, and so do I.
He'll come again,
and I know the fiddle tune.
I heard it when he came for you.

All I Want Is a Walk-On Part

Death and Other 'D' Words

Once, patients died.
Now, "resuscitation fails," or
"he shows cessation of input."
Either way the undertaker is called.
You can bet he'll never use the 'D' word.

"Mr. DoneAndGone is resting
at the Get-A-Life Funeral Parlour.
His widow will receive friends and family."
His widow? What's a guy who's only resting
doing with a widow?
If he's been doing things with someone else's widow,
no wonder he's resting.

Or the morticians announce,
"Mr. UsedToBe has passed away."
They make it sound like
he didn't pass too far away.
For another thousand bucks
they'll get him back.

When I've done my three score and ten
plus the beta blocker and by-pass eight,
don't say, "He's gone to his reward,"

or "getting what he deserves."
(Please not that!) Just say:
"He wrote tasteless doggerel about the 'D' word,
and now the damned old bugger is dead."

All I Want Is a Walk-On Part

Hospital Duty Doctor

Police often brought him in,
looked at us and smirked.
This time he stumbled in alone,
trailing the gutter
into our sterile godliness.

Defeat, stale piss and tobacco sweat
begged for help. It had never worked.
To square my conscience with refusal,
I sent him to AA, two hours early.

Half that time he'd spent
slumped in a darkened hall.
There deserts loomed,
Hell's imps taunted,
flaunted puppet strings
that made him dance the devil's jig.

Three hours later — surprise!
Olfactory *déjà vu*. He's back!
I found a bed, scrounged up food,
brief note to file: "Hopeless drunk.
DT's likely. Medications ordered.
Admit to A 5."

His unique cussedness
neutralized, tranquillized, computerized,
until next time.

He hailed me two years later on the Mall.
At first I didn't know the man,
neat guard uniform, head high,
(miracles like this can happen.)
"Thanks, doc, for trying one more time."
He firmly took my shaky hand,
and hope flowed from his palm to mine.

Prairie Scene 1968

Father, I was still young
and you were old and sick.
We stood on Temple Hill, eyes turned
to where the sky soaks up the land,
where the Voice of Thunder drums
to call the ghosts of buffalo.
It seemed I'd never looked before,
until I heard you say,
Where else could heaven be but on the prairie?

As a boy you rode your pinto
across the plains into far blue mist,
you and your cousin Lorne.
Shadows moccasined the grass
toward the spirits in the Sandy Hills:
memories of coups counted, battles fought.
You thought this would never change,
as do all boys and men — even now.

You watched the land grow old and nearly die,
plough-scarred, bleeding black soil,
ten years drought and winds
that broke men's hearts.

It healed, grew young again and new.
But fathers do not grow young
and new again, not in this place,
unless it's true, your heaven is there
invisible beside that lone cottonwood,
beyond the creek, screened by the willow trees,
where your cousin Lorne waits,
hunkered down with breechclout friends,
swapping stories by the campfire.

Southern Alberta Drought — 1934

The Model A Ford wheezed and shuddered
down the endless road
unbending as a hell-fire preacher,
toward Uncle's farm near Purple Springs,

taking me away from home,
and the cool Rockies where God lived,
and soothed His fiery beard
in the snow.

Set between my aunt and uncle
I bounced on a board,
while a bouquet of girl cousins
wilted in the back.

Dust and grasshopper clouds swirled.
Lakes dried into jig-saw patterns.
There wasn't even a mirage.
I wondered would it ever rain again.

Uncle replied,"Tonight we'll ask the Lord.
You'll join us in our family prayer."
Aunt's tight silence broke, "That'll help!
　— The Olsens prayed four years,

but lost their farm all the same.
Prayers shrivel in this devil's wind
and drift off like tumbleweed."

Still, that night we knelt and prayed.
It didn't rain.
I thought, "God lives on the mountain,
and Satan lives in Purple Springs."

The Reluctant Guest

I rudely muscled into a line of cars,
then saw that all their lights were on.
My Jeep had barged into a funeral cortege.
Traffic jammed me in, a reluctant guest
for an unplanned trip to the graveyard.

I wanted to apologize to the guest of honour,
"After you, my dear chap," I should have said.
Likely, he was pissed off like me, maybe worse,
getting stuck at a dumb party like this,
and being hauled off in a hearse.

I worked up beside the bone wagon in the lead,
as traffic thrombosed the arterial.
The undertaker saw me, did a double take.
I could have sworn he looked inside the casket,
and maybe asked, "You still with me pal?"

I had a feeling there was no one in the box.
Staring straight at me he dialled his phone,
then sirens, out to catch the truant corpse
that had the cheek to bolt and botch
the nice funeral party he had thrown.

"He's going to put me in there," I thought.
A saner mood said, "No! It's your imagination,"
but sirens closed in, I blew my cool,
walked away from the traffic constipation,
as "John Smith," checked into a small hotel.

A week later I retrieved my Jeep,
then drove to the land of broken myth.
Found the latest, still open grave.
The tombstone read, "Everyman, alias John Smith,
your resting place awaits."

Winds from the Past — Waterton 1997

For my brother and sisters, and our beloved spouses

Four retired siblings and their spouses
reminisce among the mountain pines,
drawn by shared youth.
Mother, unsure of her own role,
played many parts,
different for each child each day.
Father loved her dearly,
and each of us,
and everyone in town.

We wear age in different ways,
each touched, some bludgeoned, by tragedy.
We recall cranking the ice cream freezer,
behind the coal shed,
when jumping off the ice house
proved bravery.

Grandchildren avalanche into the cabin,
overrun our barricades,
snatch our minds back half a century,
then catapult into their van,

are gone like the years,
the years that soared like eagles,
or watched us scratch in stony ground.

...Talking, reading, playing dominoes,
unexciting pastimes for the young,
but suitable for those aware of time,
and winds that moan across the prairie snow,

or gales from underneath the world
that leech the bones and take away the light,
while a mountain breeze caresses every pine
and whispers, "Please come back another spring."

All I Want Is a Walk-On Part

Wyndham at the Breast

To my grandson, seven weeks...

This boy was screaming down the moon,
trying to kick stars from out the sky.
Now he smiles in bliss through milky lips.

Any medieval king at table,
dining with his queen above the salt,
gloating over such a groaning board,
would give his crown and counting house
for this boy's ecstasy.

Maybe the little fellow's soul,
half angel still, takes temporary leave,
wanders into Allah's scented garden,
beaming lovely visions back,
a touch and taste of paradise.
If we could market this euphoria,
packaged alluringly for adults,
the drug cartels would soon go broke.

Later, perhaps, we'll watch him land on Mars,
or hear the crowd applaud his string quartet.
Or his wife might touch his face in love,
entice his heart with her smile,

but he, with all that cornucopia,
will never find Elysian Fields again,
where once he sipped the nectar of the gods.

All I Want Is a Walk-On Part

Young Tragedian

To my grandson, Wyndham

You've learned to walk? How very quick!
Now to that clever trick you add one more.
When the world seems not to care,
you put your head down on the floor,
look up to see if eyes are on you,
open your mouth, recheck the audience,
flood those baby blues,
then seven point six on the Richter scale.

Angels in the heavens stop their play
and wring their hands at Earth's injustices.

Of course your little dramas pay,
even though the angels start to smile,
and we adults see through the ploy.
We all want people to feel sorry
and a little guilty for the way
that they, and fate, treat us,
especially a ten month boy.

I once saw Donald Wolfitt play King Lear.
That old tragedian

would have applauded your fine art.
In playing Lear he almost, very near,
put down his head upon the boards.
But sometimes in his woes and tedium,
he wished he *might* have done like you,
lay his head right down upon the floor,
while in the house, not one dry eye.

Last Retreat

I recall the smell of fresh-turned earth,
the taste of salt upon my cheeks,
I felt my muscles tense to hoist the box,
when six of us boy scouts shouldered death.

A bugle cracked and wobbled, what a farce!
Boy bugler once, now fifty years had passed,
out of breath and practice, skills all lost,
forgotten veteran of forgotten wars.

The squawking trumpet nearly made us snort,
except our coffined friend who couldn't snicker,
morticians drained his piss and vinegar,
and syringed embalmer's fluid through his heart.

Maybe in heaven he'll bedevil the lord,
or else in hell, lord it over the devil,
so there it ended with a prayer, a shovel,
and old defeated trumpeter's last retreat.

The grave exhaled its musty odours,
Our friend couldn't hear the bugle bleat,
nor smell the farmer's cow manure and sweat,
nor see nor touch their lovely daughters.

Spring's Prairie Oratorio

Down the sunny coulee's bank
a tiny trickle, *sotto voce*,
rises to a drum roll.
Chinook, old *maestro*,
rolls back the snow.

Gophers, blinking at the light,
run up and down the scale,
to warm up for the fanfare.

Excited birds in party dress
arrive back just in time,
as a cummerbunded robin
taps his baton.

Glee clubs of blue birds
rush in and sing of crocuses.
Meadow larks exalt every valley.

The whole world stands
for *The Hallelujah Chorus*.

All I Want Is a Walk-On Part

I wish I could just walk into life,
and on a crummy day like this,
walk out and slam the door,
and later, maybe tomorrow or next week
I'd walk into life somewhere else.

No telling when I'd come back,
so I wouldn't have promises to keep,
the main things I'd turn my back on,
instead of getting mad at myself
for making any in the first place.

I'd like to take you when I walk,
but it wouldn't work:
You pride yourself on keeping promises,
and even make some for me to keep....

So while you're doing promise-duty,
I'll walk out and cool it,
wherever one rests after a long walk,
when he can't face another wedding or funeral,
especially my own.

There's one promise I'd walk out on for sure
and walk in somewhere else.

Cottage Phantoms

Through screens of sumac
time-chiselled rock edges the lake,
logs sculptured into totems.

The loon laments forgotten gods.
Here is pain of all lost lovers' dreams:
unseen spirits watch another generation
kneel to wild flowers florid as the sunset.

Gulls shimmer pink above the lake,
sails luff in tight-lipped wind,
insects water dance.

Phantoms sigh. Toward the dusk
fades our canoe,
soon gone into the dark.

Night speaks. From vanished years
our childrens' chatter jumbles with pagan cries —
our whispers blend with lost voices.

AGMV
MARQUIS
Québec, Canada
2000